Shouting At 1
Vol: 1 Shells

Pablo Doherty

ISBN: 1507852401
ISBN-13 : 9781507852408

DEDICATION

For Mary Kate & the kids

CONTENTS

72 Zzzzzzz

Angel's Cove

There's a little piece of heaven
Near the town of Donaghamore
Where memories are so cherished
As you enter through the door

Such genuine affection
And a wish to understand
There's an atmosphere of caring
From an ever helping hand

No tale or thought is worthless
And this family love to hear
For the people and their story's
Are the precious souvenirs

Let us dance like Ginger Rodgers
In the arms of Fred Astaire
As we laugh at Laurel n Hardy
That piano and the stairs

And at times we may remember
At the closing of the day
Close friends we had in war time
Who now have passed away

No book is ever ended
For the sun will never set
On the hope we found in Corkhill
And the friends that we have met

Arthur Crump

Look at the face on Arthur Crump
The grumpiest boy in town
You'd think he found a tenner
Then lost a hundred pound

When he was born in Belfast town
At last I had a brother
But when the doctor saw his face
He turned and slapped his mother

Young Arthur is a keen sportsman
At soccer he is great
Though when he scored a goal today
He wouldn't celebrate

At school the teachers rave about
His Maths and English lit
But when our Art got greatest child
He didn't care a bit

But what is this is it a smile
Beginning to appear
A strangely upturned frown
That goes from ear to ear

Ah now I see the reason why
Young Arthur's looking smug
The dog has just boked up his lunch
On mummy Persian rug

Ava

Commotion in the tea room
Draws me to the door
I shuffle past excited crowd
In order to see more

A beaming smile of happiness
Is fixed on mothers face
The child plays to her audience
With confidence and grace

Outstretched arms await the chance
To hold this child of God
Then with a cheeky knowing look
She says " I'm Ava Todd"

"My mum and dad have waited
And now they are complete
I'm feeling like a princess
Who's on a meet and greet"

This world is so much bigger
So much for me to see
I heard them talking in the car
Of a place called Disney

So mum I won't grow up too fast
And we will take our time
For if your ever feeling down
Just put your hand in mine

Beard

You've changed how others look at me
As you sit upon my skin
And add a touch of eloquence
To an otherwise bare chin

In truth it's hard to recollect
A time before you came
We've grown close for several weeks
And now I'm not the same

To walk alone without your touch
Would feel so out of place
I think you complement my style
And warm my ageing face

It's been a journey full of views
Some pleasant, others less
At times with razor in my hand
I've questioned your success

So settle in, your here to stay
I'll keep you trim and neat
Your blend of "ginger shades of grey"
Has made my look complete

So lads and lords around the globe
Give yourself some flare
Leave your BICS upon the shelf
And grow some facial hair

Bernie

The smell of scented petals
Greets your journeys end
With open arms you feel the warmth
Of your guide and trusted friend

Her prayer is your companion
Wherever you should roam
Life's daily toil and turmoil
Are absent in her home

Her dreams are of the family
Who have flown from the nest
She has sent them out into the world
And told them "do your best"

With words so full of comfort
To those when times are tough
That help us tread the rocky path
By smoothing out the rough

And though at times life's hardships
Have visited her door
Her faith has stretched its hand out
To raise her from the floor

At festive family feasting
She gathers in her young
Protecting, ever giving
With a heart engulfed with fun

She welcomes friends and neighbours
With a non-judgmental hand
And differing opinions
She strives to understand

Such complete dedication
To our children she displays
And in her eyes reflected
Are thoughts of distant days

Bike

Historically I've criticised
The helmet wearing crew
Who spent their time on country roads
Blocking me and you

For in the car you'd hear me roar
At cycle groups of three or four
As my frustration they'd ignore
From Lurgan Town to the Lough shore

All shapes and sizes can be seen
In fiery pink and emerald green
As sons and fathers are squeezed in
To figure hugging Lycra skin

They all seek pleasure from the thrill
Of peddling quickly down steep hill
Sharpe corners pose a threat to few
At traffic lights they sail on through

Now to you all I must confess
I've laughed at those in Wiggins dress
And failed at times to see the fun
Of leather seat on chunky bum

So tell the world I've changed my ways
Pablo's got two wheels
Though just for now the gear can wait
Till the Lycra pant he feels

Brian

We've just been adopted
By a great big ginger cat
Who arrived here on a Monday
I think something like that

His teeth must be the biggest
That I've ever seen
And his eyes they are the colour
Of piercing emerald green

He sits on our back window
And cries out all day long
It really is annoying
Like a bad X factor song

He follows us around the place
When we go to the car
And when we come home later on
He is never that far

We've decided that we'll call him Brian
And he answers back to that
Brian the great big gingered
Emerald eyed cat

Buttered Toast

Surely nothing can compare
To toasted wafting in the air
For when fresh butter meets it's host
And you bite firmly on your toast

Then raise your eyes and nod your head
In appreciation that your grilled bread
Has eased the journey from your bed
And brightened up your day instead

As crumbs take flight in words you said
And land on paper that is read
Now with the last round son has fled
So to the cupboard stare in dread

In tears i fall upon the floor
As with the treasure out the door
"Ones not enough" I crave for more
Of white with creamy fresh Dromore

Caravan Holiday in Donegal

With ghostly howl of frantic midnight wind
She rattles through the shell in which we sit
Searching for an entry where to strike
In silence we await the storm to hit

Lightning strikes it's match across the sky
In textbook Hitchcock cinematic style
Every creak and whistle magnified
I fear it will be with us for a while

On glass eclipsed by steam from our still breath
Rain drops pave their way from left to right
We sit and feast on chocolate mallow treats
That obviously will feel no heat tonight

A crash of timber prompts a nervous laugh
What act of madness brought us to this place
In secret prayer we hide our inner fear
And search for comfort in our flame lit face

The night engulfs us whole and pounds its heart
It strokes a hand of chill upon our skin
We wait on tender hooks it's wrath to fall
Then draws she back as we retreat within

Conversation with Lorcan on Dun Laoghaire Pier

What if that sea gull swept down from the sky
And lifted me way out to sea
What would you do dad
To come to my aid
How would you rescue me?

I'd grab that lads fishing rod
Out of his hand
And hook that old gull by its beak
Then quicker than you could shout
"Dippers for tea"
I'd have you back safe on your feet

What if a monster rose up from the deep
And crashed its tail onto this pier
What would you do dad
To keep us both safe
How would we flee from here?

I'd hold that big sea serpent
Tight in my hands
Till it's silvery scales turn to blue
Then I'd throw it away
Back into the waves
I'm telling you, that's what I'd do

What if an alien space ship appeared
With little green men all inside
What would you do dad
To chase them away
Where could we run and hide?

Well little green men, they are scared of your dad
For I fought them on Space Planet nine

Ok I was younger and faster on foot
And had one or two glasses of wine

What if some pirates took over that boat
And threatened to sail it away
What would you do dad
To make them come back
How would you make them stay?

I say to them " lads you've got ten to get out"
For the Garda are just on their way
They've stopped for some ice cream at Teddy's bazaar
And are heading straight for Dublin Bay

"What are they getting at Teddy's bazaar?"
"Ice cream? did I hear you say"
What a fantabulous idea of yours
To complete a wonderful day
Let's go!

Countryside Wine Disaster

These words I give to you have been inspired
From one for whom wine is now required
Who spilt the nectar hence on the floor
And thus is heading off throughout the door

Though spare a little thought for those like me
Who don't possess the pleasant luxury
Of walking distance wine selling Offee
And face a night of complete misery

Ok so I do choose to live in style
With no ale house within distance of a mile
And nor can I drive to the nearest Town
This now ruled out as I have two tins down

So I hold strong and tightly to my glass
I pray your vino drought will quickly pass
And wine to lips act I will try to master
We'll have no countryside wine disaster

Crisps

I love the cheesy Quaver
With it's curves and curly style
Its crunchy at the first bite
Then fluffy for a while
The flavour lasts forever
Which always makes me smile
When I kiss a Quaver raver
It's like fireworks on the Nile

The Min Chip that's barbecued
Is a costly little treat
It's difficult to find this gem
In most shops on the street
It's not first choice for many
When you question those you meet
But when that beef burst hits your throat
It knocks you off your feet

Tayto Cheese n Onion
Is a favourite over here
Many get through several packs
When drinking German beer
They've even got their own theme park
Folks come from far and near
And students based in England
Import loads every year

Golden Wonder Ready Salted
Are welcome through my door
But when finishing my first blue bag
I always reach for more
Though tempted by my lovely wife
Other flavours to explore
By half past eight on Friday night
I'm salted to the core

Hula Hoops are practical
They fit neatly in the lunch
There's spicy, pickled onion
And beef flavoured Monster Munch
When buying something for the kids
I always have a hunch
A multi flavoured maxi pack
Will fill my hungry bunch

Cure

I walk bare skin on dampened land
To blow the Guinness from my pore
At one with water air and sand
My mind on sea bird wing does sore

My thoughts released of worldly woe
And clear to picture natures tide
The last few days I will forgo
And flee the truth they try to hide

Morning breeze does clear the way
For gentle ripple from the deep
This time alone I will hold dear
New memories for me to keep

I will return to where I was
Drift gently into my routine
Reflect upon the path I take
My cure is only but a dream

Day Off With Lorcan

The boredom ate away at him
As rust on a sunken hull
He'd feigned a morning headache
And conned a day off school

By ten his skull was bursting
From just sitting in his room
His mind with thoughts was racing
In dispersed with static gloom

"There hasn't been a nose bleed
In our class for near a year"
As a little head peaks round the door
And the patient does appear

"This being sick is rubbish
When you have no friends around"
"Did you know we're not allowed to run
When out in the playground"

"My tummy's feeling better now
Though it's rumbling all the time
I think some crispy bacon
Would make it quite sublime"

By noon he's got the pillows
And the duvet from his bed
There's cartoons on the telly
He is content and fed

Ellen

She runs to me
Excitement lights up in her every breathing word
That fills my heart with over bursting pride
I want to hold her up and tell the world

No words can I release upon the air
That paints for thee the love only a father knows
When by her acts you realise your dreams
Reflect the generosity she shows

Sometimes it is too easy to be lost
We shout loudest in order to be heard
Our cries to find our role in family life
Is hardest for the child who is born third

Forgive me Ellie if your cries today I fail to hear
To lose a daughters love my greatest fear
And run to me if ever in your life
You find yourself in trouble, need or strife.

Excessive Sound

I strode into work today
And gathered all around
To test the theory put to me
That I made excessive sound

All giggled with amusement
At the tale you did relay
How every breath and grunt and groan
Did fill you with dismay

So pretty darling Mary Kate
I make this pledge to thee
I'll stick my lips together
when your watching Sky TV

No crunching of my nuts
Nor smacking of my lips
Will make you pull your hair out
Or leave you mind in bits

So if you hear a grunting
In the very dead of night
Fear not it's just old Pablo
Who's lungs are getting tight

He's no longer a spring chicken
And his bones are getting old
His mid night jerky movements
Are a symptom of the cold

But when it comes to loving
Don't you ever scoff
Until the day poor Pablo's
Light is finally turned off!

Farewell To Beal Feirste

Farewell to Beal Feirste
Town of my youth
To where many a story was spoke
I'm sailing away from the Emerald Isle
For my body is old and I'm broke

Many girls have been kissed
And I've promised to write
To the family i leave behind
I'm heading to England to earn me a pay
God only knows what I'll find

I'm leaving the land which has made me a man
And I bring with me only a dream
That someday I'll return to the place of my birth
And relay all the wonders I've seen

So farewell to Beal Feiste
Your brown terraced home
Will stay with me all of my days
I'll picture your welcome wherever I roam
I'll miss you in so many ways

Fatherhood

I have reached my own conclusion
To this organised confusion
Though in maintaining this illusion
May require a brain transfusion

Father's nerves are slowly bruising
From the grip that he is loosing
On the life that they are choosing
And his advice they are refusing

And they find it so amusing
His need to hide in weekend boozing
"Leave him kids" says Mum diffusing
"Quiet now" daddy's snoozing

Fatherhood (Part II)

Do not wake sweet prince for bravely you have fought
Far too many battles on this day
The Queen is tired and taken to her bed
The King is feeling old and looking grey

You quelled rebellious foe on ASDA floor
By verbalising threats and kicking door
The candy treasure raised aloft so high
Inflicting scorn on nosy passer-by

And when the X-box battle you did fight
Through most of day and well into the night
Never once did you give up your right
And gripped controller one with all your might

And yes my prince I do have to confess
That I was far too slow in meeting your request
For chocolate covered wheat flakes to digest
If only with four arms I could be blessed

So sleep my prince and paint a picture in your dream
Of love and joy and happiness that you bring
As tightly to my palm your fingers cling
Your ever loyal father, friend and King

Fishing Off Rocks For Conger Eels

Fishing off rocks for conger eels
With Scotty and the three O'Neills
Sea weed tightly gripped our heels
Weighed down with rods, hooks, floats and reels
We stopped ourselves from falling

In holidays and after school
We clambered over rock and pool
As crashing waves met foreland
We faced them down and made our stand
We stopped ourselves from falling

With rehearsed arm flicking motion
Cast our lines into the ocean
As shouts and laughter filled the air
Sea spray drenched the young friend's hair
We stopped ourselves from falling

No conger eel was hooked that day
We hurried home without delay
As North Sea wave caressed the rock
A tidal race against the clock
We stopped ourselves from falling

Old friends have gone their separate ways
Our memories formed from older days
Now lines are cast with kith and kin
As new life journey's we begin
We stop ourselves from falling

Float

Wish me peace as I float from old into the new
And believe me that I wish no suffering on you
I did not have the will nor strength to fight
Days within my mind were dark as night

This shell I leave with you please lay to rest
Place my picture high upon the wall
Speak of me when I was at my best
And know your arms so often broke my fall

The preacher tells me of a Holy place
Before this gate I come to pay my toll
I offer up my innocence and pain
And place into His arms my wounded soul

So lay my coffin lowly in the earth
And know my spirit dances on the wind
Wish me peace as I float from old into this new
And believe that I wished no suffering on you

Fox Lake

She let the emerald linen
Rest a moment in her palm
Amidst the evening chorus
Her thoughts were still and calm

To the distant hills of Donegal
She felt desire to roam
With the Swilly breeze upon her face
In the land that she called home

As the moon lit painted colours
Skipped like fireflies o're Fox Lake
Her memories still fondest
Of her time on summer break

Though American by accent
There's a heart from Erin's isle
As she thinks about her relatives
She gives a little smile

For she recalls time in Ireland
In the town land of Dunree
As she walked in mother's footsteps
And touched her family

Then that nervous chance encounter
When Jim came and asked her name
She knew that from that first breath
Life would never be the same

As they faced the world together
In this land across the foam
They embraced the new world challenge
In the place they would call home

She then closed her eyes to savour
As the laughter filled the air
And felt their love reflected
In all who gathered there

Eight Irish sons and daughters
Jim and Mary's gift to all
They extend the warmest welcome
When relatives do call

Then her children came around her
Took the linen from her grasp
"We'll look forward to the future mum,
But not forget the past"

Friendship

In these days of global stardom
And the multi-millionaire
Idolising of great sportsmen
Sleeve tattoos and spiky hair

Inflated match day tickets
Are inflicted on loyal fans
Who'll spend their hard earned wages
For a seat among the stands

Through the darkened Bentley windows
Fall the cries, the shouts and screams
For a quick glimpse of our hero's
Who are team mates in our dreams

And the loyal masses question
How the thirst for fame they quench
As the agent and the player
Check their shares while on the bench

But an incident has happened
That put superstars to shame
When a Greek lad we call Georgie
Borough respect back to the game

By a simple act of friendship
He immortalised the day
When he shunned the flashing cameras
And sought out his friend Jay

With the flags and scarfs all waving
Georgie held his pal up high
And Jay's smile and pure excitement
Touched the clouds up in the sky

As the image of this friendship
Beamed on all our tv screens
Jay and Georgie's day together
Will live long in football dreams

Gerry

I sat at traffic lights this morn
And heard the the sad news break
Of the passing of our finest son
Old Gerry "Turkey neck"

He's hung his mike upon the stand
We'll hear his crac no more
He'll spin the discs in heaven now
And make the angels roar

He eased the pain of daily life
Ran boat trips down the Foyle
Found bits and bobs for country folk
Urged on by Seany Coyle

He loved the tales of long ago
Show bands and dance hall nights
He wagged the chin with famous folk
Daniel and all the like

He found the little cats and dogs
Of Belfast's girls and boys
Who sat in silence by the phone
Squeezing squeaky toys

So Gerry thanks for all the laughs
You've brightened many hearts
Cheered up old men in smokey bars
And located old car parts

Halloween

"Ahhhhh" screamed the boy
In fearful dread
As he felt the grip of Dr Dead
Pull him from his cosy bed
His fangs so sharpe
And lips so red

His blankets fell
Upon the floor
As he was dragged
Toward the door
"HELP ME MUM" the lad did roar
But she could help her son no more

For on her flesh
The beast had tore
And from her neck
The blood did pore
Now she his bride
For ever more

His tiny fingers grabbed at wall
Then down the stairs
The lad did fall
And from below with final stare
He saw the cape
The slicked back hair

He summoned up
A strength within
He searched for hope
In kitchen bin
At last he had a stroke of luck
And garlic chicken he did pluck

Then with two chopsticks
Crossed in hand
He chased the beast
Back to his land
And on his doorstep he did stand
Not quite the day that he had planned

Hippy Me

Tightened grip on steering wheel
Rain washed traffic bars my way
As frustration slowly builds
I tread another hectic day

The constant drill of mobile phone
In eighties synthesiser beat
With endless dull monotonous tone
I grunt at those in hall I meet

Then from safety of the car
A target for this life dismay
As temper gathers pace inside
I spy the bearded grey hippy

He saunters by without a care
War green bandana on his head
He knows not of work despair
No doubt on way home to his bed

This ageless social politic
Shoulder hair, unwashed and wild
Badge clad message on lapel
A dinosauric sixties child

I stare at beaded happy man
Who worries not if bills are missed
"Socialist Worker" on his shirt
Political with ironic twist

I slowly down the window wind
And from my salivating gob
Shout at him in angry tone
"Oi hippy, go and get a job"

Then in view of mirrored glass
My reflection I do catch
Without the clothes and facial hair
I and the Hippy perfect match

My youth had quietly passed me by
With slight of hand I have become
Against all my rebellious cries
A product of my Dad and Mum

My children all now stare at me
With muffled word and shaken head
I stand in busy street alone
Repeating words my parents said!

I Cannot Sleep

Though I am tired I cannot sleep
As morning sky does gently creep
Against the clock my heart does beat
Resigned to ultimate defeat

My crib tonight is incomplete
I am at war with blasted heat
For head is hot but not are feet
As duvet rests in tangled heap

My mind does race with thoughts so deep
Appointments I have yet to keep
Again, again, repeat, repeat
Of those whom I am supposed to meet

The distant cry of feline weep
Floats softly down the silent street
But twisting, turning cannot reap
Success in battle with this sheet

My wife does breath in slumber sweet
She knows not of the tears I weep
As I grow evermore so weak
And drift at last to blissful sleep

Jean to Slack

I have made the smooth transition
From a comfortable position
To which I fear can't turn back
I've moved myself from Jean to slack

Without a sign of going there
The cotton slack I love to wear
In brown or blue but never black
My rear is snug and quite compact

You all will say I'm getting old
To make a fashion move so bold
Though when I open up the door
The navy slack I can't ignore

My wife responded with some venom
When I turned my rear from denim
But now I get a loving smack
When I wear my mustard slack

Advice I give to everyone
With stone washed denim on their bum
Leave Levi's to the younger pack
And move your rear from jean to slack!

Left Behind

It is with gentle peace of mind
I think of those I've left behind
And softly float with style and grace
Into His caring safe embrace

I leave my memory for to hold
As comfort should the times grow cold
And watch with pride from up above
As you spread happiness and love

With pride I'll speak of those I leave
Allowing them some time to grieve
But to the angels I'll recall
My years of laughter with you all

Of how I held on as you walked
Proclaimed to all when you first talked
And kissed your bruises when you fell
Such conversations I will tell

So say hello to me each day
I'll never be too far away
And pretty soon I'm sure you'll find
I'm watching those I've left behind

Lonely Tractor Sunday Night

The fall of steam on bathroom glass
And drift of Old Spice in the air
The hateful drone of "Wagon Wheel"
I can but stand in lost despair

As last weeks folded "Country Life"
Tied up in knots upon the fire
He called me darling all day long
Then ran and left me in this mire

He'll scrub all sign of dirt from skin
And hide the truth he works the land
Then with his cohorts scan the room
To catch the gentle painted hand

Then with arms around her waist
Will dance till close on sawdust floor
And as they part her kiss he'll taste
Then home to me he'll come once more

And he will need me in the morning
Call me darling, treat me right
But now I am a lonely tractor
And it is still a Sunday night

Middle Girth, It's Time To Go

The trainers have been whitened
The track suite hung to dry
I've checked the road conditions
And looked up at the sky

I've polished off the chocolates
Crisps and lemonade
Informed friends and family
Of the pledge that I have made

Downloaded applications
Regulated my heartbeat
Taken all precautions
Relating to my feet

Set myself a target
For whatever that it's worth
To be a 32' again
Around my middle girth

Asked for help from Jesus
The wife, and those I meet
To help me stem this flowing tide
And weeble type physique

I know it's not the first time
I've fought the dreaded flab
But what's reflected back at me
Is droopy, pale and sad

So throw out pies and pudding
Ice cream goes in the bin
No lovely treats shall pass my lips
Until I'm nice and thin

Mind your language da!

Two new tyres for mummy car
And the heatings on the blink
No sky tv in the local bar
There's a drip below the sink

The garden fence has blown down
There's a fuel bill on the mat
Fifty pound for a dental crown
Sterilise the cat

Late own goal against the bhoys
School fees eighty quid
Lorcan crying broken toys
Over tightened lid

Car keys lost at five to nine
No T- bags in the tin
That last choc pop, it was mine
They didn't lift the bin

The grass needs cut I'm going grey
You need to phone your ma
Finger closed in the cupboard door
"Mind your language da!"

My Get Up And Go Has Got Up And Gone

I need a zest transfusion
A new and fresh approach
I feel so disillusioned
I need a lifestyle coach

My wardrobe needs ejecting
I'm wearing 90's brands
My hair is getting thinner
And staying on my hands

The music's getting louder
I'm reading cookery books
The kids no longer share my jokes
And give me dirty looks

I use to have the magic
I knew the chat to use
My moves upon the dance floor
Left them dazed and quite confused

Now I groove in kitchens
On birthdays with the kids
It's Little Mix and Ga Ga
Not Madness or The Skids

Our Maz is scared and worried
She asks " is something wrong?"
I say I've lost my 'get up'
I think it's upped and gone

But wait I have an idea
To reignite my life
My 'get ups' only sleeping
I better wake the wife.........oops

My Son Don't Find Me Funny Anymore

My son don't find me funny anymore
He just says "Wise up dad and close the door"
And doesn't even ask me " What's the score"
Proclaiming "watching footballs such a bore".

My son he used to laugh and joke about
Especially when his mother use to shout
But now he yells at me "OK, MAN JUST GET OUT"
And makes a face with raised eyes and a pout

My son would hold my hand when in the street
And be polite to people we would meet
But now he just stands staring at his feet
And gives a grunting huff as if to greet

I miss my little buddy more each day
How he would look at me and softly say
"Oh daddy won't you come outside and play"
The sun is shining on this wondrous day

Now it's hard to get him off the chair
He's lost his boyish looks and stylish flare
Replaced them with a patronising stare
His favourite phrase is "really, I don't care!"

So all of you who sit and feel my pain
Please say he'll be my little boy again
I think I'm going gradually insane
I know it is the parents they will blame!

North West 200

On a wee dark road on the shores of the Bann
Sit four wet men in a transit van
Mick and Tom and Pat and Dan
Heating beans in a frying pan

Says Mick to Tom I wont be back
To this here bloody racing track
Me legs are soaked and so's me back
This North West 200 ain't much crac

Says Pat to Mick as he shakes his head
"This road racing's all but dead
We'll hey tae stay wi the wives instead"
Which filled the other three with dread

So on that night they hatched a plot
And two by four in bulk was sought
And the four without a thought
Built a roof around the lot

"We'll start at the pits" now that's the plan
Said Mick to Pat and Tom and Dan
"You dig the holes" said Pat to Mick
"I'll get to laying out the brick"

" Dan, lay the felt and cut it thick"
Said Tom as he he dug holes with Mick
"And don't forget to brew the tea"
Said Dan back to the other three

The worked all night through hurt and pain
From York corner till Coleraine
Through Metro pole and back again
In wind and dark and chill and rain

As the bikers woke next day
And met dark skies with much dismay
"Ney racing sham" were heard to say
"Let's head back hame without delay"

But our four lads had other plans
And welcomed out the tented shams
To see the roof along the track
That brought their hairy grins all back

"It's those four builders from Strabane"
"The ones in the oul transit van"
"They've saved the Nor West" said one man
Thanks Pat and Mick and Tom and Dan!

Ode To The Portstewart Fisherman

From early morn at harbours wall
We watched the boats come back
As pipe tobacco filled the air
The catch they would unpack

And offer up to our young hands
The bounty from their night
And those the fishers could not sell
Hung lifeless from our bike

I watched as mother held the fish
Then with a surgeons skill
She slit the skin from mouth to tail
And placed it on the grill

Then in my teens I did serve pints
In a pub at the break of day
Where tales were told ore stout n' eggs
Of the one that got away

I heard of men who rode the wave
Brothers, sons and friends
Of lives that rest beyond the wall
Fishers to the end

So hail to those who brave the seas
And cast their nets each day
May Saint Peter keep a watchful eye
And safely guide your way

Portfamous

You could hear the shouts of children
And the sound of slot machines
As the litter blew so freely
In the streets they seldom clean

For the folks travelled in train loads
Just to ride the Dipper high
And to drink along the sea front
As they watched the world go by

Squeezed like sardines into swimwear
Wearing plastic bowler hats
Asking strangers for affection
"Kiss me quick" and things like that

But they seldom ventured westward
From the flashing lights and bells
They came not for natural beauty
Just night clubs and chippy smells

And the occasional day tripper
Who came to stray our way
Stood bewildered at the harbour
Then quickly drove away

And I doubt they even noticed
As they strolled along the prom
That the sunset on the coastline
Inspired bold Jimmy's song

Or that sitting on a deck chair
At the front of that hotel
Was a legendary hero
With a Munich tale to tell

As they moved among the traffic
Wishing for the Belfast streets
They passed Morrelli's cafe
And it's world renowned iced treats

Then up towards the Diamond
Could they really understand
The artistic wealth of talent
That walked out towards the strand

That world established comic
We all know as young Jimeoin
Liked his stout poured in the Anchor
And calls Portstewart his home

And never mind The Beautiful South
The North Coast's fine as well
As Briana with her number one
Was often heard to tell

Its so good to hear the news these days
In a brog we understand
For Ann Marie and Sarah
Are also from this land

Did they ever look for music
Out the back of Murphy's bar
To see "our" good old Henry
The most famous son by far

So I say to you sun seeker
As your sitting on the bus
For a more cultural experience
Take a look at Portfamous

Portstewart Rocks

A flame haired man once said to me
As we were looking out to sea
Words so wise he did decree
To set us on our life's journey

We sat on rocks with tin in hand
And planned to leave our native land
The dreams we had were ours to make
To win, to loose, to build, to break

"Pablo my friend
Here is the deal
Two boats in the harbour
But one for sail"

Then with a swig, a laugh, a smile
We sat in silence for a while
Then threw our ladies to the deep
And parted with those words to keep

Years have gone by but memory not
And all my dreams I now have got
Yet still we can't turn back the clocks
Drinking with Haughey on Portstewart rocks.

Puberty, (so much to answer for!)

I think the real intention
Of Dr Frankenstein's machine
Was not rebirth of normality
But more creation of a teen

This strange bemusing subject
All dishevelled when awoke
With pimple bursting attitude
From every breath that's spoke

As we ponder through life's issues
And the magnitude of space
The path we took through puberty
Put all others in their place

They once were our wee baby's
All powder, sweet and light
Who reached out tiny fingers
For us to clutch at night

They toddled round the garden
And we grinned with naive pride
As with dribbled spits said "Mammy"
Something sprung for joy inside

The petrified expression
As you kissed them off to school
Now they run without a mention
For a sad rejected fool

They ponder over menus
When you give yourself a break
It's no longer chicken dippers
It's all starters and a steak

Then they use the flippin en suite
As a place to style their hair
And I'm forced to read the paper
In the cold one neath the stair

It's all Xbox points and FIFA
Zombie flesh, Assassins Creed
Call of Duty black ops
And bloody Need for Speed

Without any rhyme or reason
They'll amaze you with their wit
Then they damn your name forever
If you point out one wee zit

Oh puberty the web you weave
Has put many to the pen
To explain youths complication
As they move from boys to men

Reflections From A Condemned Bird

High up on the kitchen wall
The clock reads five past seven
My cousin Henry left me here
Carried off to turkey heaven

He lived a proud and happy life
In the garden out the back
Now his guts are in the bin
Wrapped up in a clean film pack

I must be still, here comes the boss
It looks as though she's huffing
She's peeling spuds and cutting veg
And laying out the stuffing

Well, here we go what's happening
Hey, gently show some care
You could have warmed your hands up love
Before you put them there

Now where's this place I'm going to
That's where she cooks the meat
Hey Ms Doyle relax yourself
Easy on the heat

It's getting very warm in here
My skin is going crispy
I'm nearly flaming roasting dear
Life's looking pretty risky

The table's set with festive treats
Cranberry sauce and crackers
Brussels, carrots, butter beans
And roasties by my knackers

There's music on and candles lit
As the banquet comes alive
Beaming faces, hungry hordes
As I finally arrive

"I'll have a leg" "It's breast for me"
Gravy, mash and peas
There's always loads to go around
Carve me gently please

Reflecting in my final hours
I lived a simple life
And now I sit in pride of place
"Crikey mind that knife"

Shadows

It seemed like only yesterday
We gathered in this place
And watched with trepidation
The shadows on your face

And how apologetic
As the news you did recall
And swore to fight what lay ahead
Your pain was felt by all

In weeks and months that followed
We spoke and thought of you
The strength within your family
We hoped would help you through

Appointments were attended
The treatment did begin
And if life at times looked dark
You found a strength within

Now here you sit among us
With your mother by your side
The light that once was going dim
Is beaming bright with pride

The path you walked was rocky
And you'll wish not to retrace
Let your journey be a strength for those
With a shadow on their face

Shells

Come, arch your back and curl into the sand
Like shells we hide our face from blown grain
No wind can coil it's spell upon our skin
Our youth will keep us shielded from the rain

Block out the cries for you to hasten home
In fear we may be caught within the storm
You have no wish to leave your coral hide
For in your shell it's safe, secure and warm.

Then under much direction from my son
I arched my back and curled into the sand
Closed my eyes and listened to the gales
At once I was a shell on Portstewart strand

I heard waves break like thunder on the shore
The seagulls beg the fisher for his trawl
I felt the wind go whistling through my hair
As heavy rain upon this shell did fall

This is the greatest gift a child can give
To let you see the world from where they stand
I urge you if caught out within a storm
Curl up and be a shell upon the sand

Shouting At the Sea

Open up the doors
Set the demons free
Exercise your social stress
By shouting at the sea

Frustrated by your lack of power
Or the cruelty of life
Take a deck chair to the beach
And verbalise your strife

If feeling that the one you love
Just fails to understand
Move your troubles to the coast
And leave them on the sand

So venture up to Donegal
If you ever disagree
And join me on the golden shore
Shouting at the sea.

Teenage Nights In Kelly's

On Friday nights when school was ore
With Kestrel in our belly's
We donned our finest stay pressed slacks
And headed off to Kelly's

Drenched in Old Spice from our dads
And dressed in God knows what
We met on rocks for "carry outs"
Then took the three mile walk

From our "wee Port" till Kelly's bar
Seemed like the longest day
With several can's of three percent
To help us on our way

Oh what a feast of teenage fun
Lay beyond the door
St Joe's and Convent stayed downstairs
High School and Inst, top floor

As Gerry mixed up Indi tracks
With heavy U.S funk
Upstairs they danced to Chaka Khan
And supped on fizzy plonk

Those brief liaisons down the back
And we didn't ask their name
A friend of someone's sister
Sure it's all part of the game

Then after seven pints of stout
A welcome break was needed
We waded through each other's pee
Hygiene just went unheeded

Four hours of endless alcohol
A bit of shy flirtation
Then off we headed home again
And dreamy contemplation

Terezita

No doubt she'll wake with swollen head
Her body numbed with pain
And swear she'll give up partying
To never drink again

She slowly rise from slumber deep
And walk the bathroom tile
Throw water onto delicate skin
Then grin a cheeky smile

She look into the mirrored glass
And groan at what is there
A mishmash mass of tangled mess
That once was sculptured hair

She take the brush out from the drawer
A pull it this and that
She'll wet and gel and colour up
And maybe try a hat

She invest pounds and penny's
On sprays and dyes and clips
And when she has it as she likes
She'll change the way it sits

Now I have watched for many hours
Seen styles both long and short
Her extensions and the curly phase
Without uttering a thought

But now as you reach twenty
And no longer are a teen
I sit hear with receding hair
All envious and green

Dear daughter Terezita
Your a NATURAL beauty queen
You don't need fake cosmetics
For your portrait to be seen

The image that is glowing
From the path you chose to walk
Will keep the heads a turning
And make the people talk

So smile back in the mirror
And as you say stay strong
There'll always be a place for you
That's safe secure and warm

The 12th of July: a memory

With beat of drum and whistling flute
In bowler hat and coloured suit
We crouch down with curtain drawn
For most of day from early morn

With curious care neath window sill
Watch open eyed in nervous chill
We are disturbed and called away
And told to "Let them have their day"

As we play cards on back room floor
There is a knock upon the door
We stare in silence at each other
Then to the kitchen goes our mother

A well-dressed man of rural sort
Advises her he's been caught short
He speaks to her with humble grace
Pressure etched upon his face

He enters room and greets us all
Sees Sacred Heart upon the wall
Then with an act of some respect
His sash from collar he does take

As he departs he wished us well
And left us with this tale to tell
How with some mutual give and take
The Orangeman got a welcome break

The Belfast Busker

He stands alone in afternoon
With bearded face and three note tune
A solo act, on stone grey street
With grandad's hat beside his feet

He plays to audience of four
And those who gather in shop door
To flee the crowds or have a smoke
With passers bye he shares a joke

He sings of men with broken dreams
Brown eyed girls and dancing queens
Of those who sailed to foreign shore
And walk the Belfast streets no more

Through darker times he plied his trade
In Corn Market and Queens Arcade
As smoke and tear gas filled the air
He played guitar without a care

Neath helicopter in the sky
He belted Don's American Pie
And when the bomb scare siren came
He moved along, then sang again

A steadfast symbol of our past
Who played through riot, fire and blast
To normalise and entertain
Us all, regardless of their name

The Bright Nights Do Play Havoc

The bright nights do play havoc
With our young and active minds
For daylight still, as lasers beam
From the cracks between the blinds

Father cuts the grass out front
As the daylight starts to fade
We toss and turn and battle sleep
Gainst the purring rotary blade

The sound of conversation
Draws us up to catch our ear
And frees us from the tangled sheets
Familiar tones to hear

The written words of comic slant
Fail to keep our eye
Young minds are like blank canvas
As the air is warm and dry

The bark of dog and stack of cup
Are amplified below
As daily toys are packed away
The eyelids heavy grow

One last hurrah, a cry for juice
Will help us close the day
Recharge our bones and little minds
To dreams we drift away

The Death of The Bullshitter

I must bring to your attention
An issue of concern
The art of bullshit died today
And never will return

In every public house and bar
An empty seat will sit
Where once the local bullshitter
Would charm us with his wit

But now he is redundant
And very seldom out
For every pearl of wisdom
Is greeted with some doubt

Your granddad played for Arsenal
Quick tell me what's his name?
Ill check it out on Google
To verify your claim

It saddens me to see the end
Of such a social art
I feel the worlds a lesser place
Since the bullshit did depart

The Gate Inn

By the Lough Neagh shore on a windy night
I stumbled through the door
Of a bar full of men with a tale to tell
And sawdust on the floor

I nodded my head to a guy with a beard
Then shook from my hair the rain
I stood by the fire to warm my bones
And the landlord spoke his name

"They call me Brian I'm the boss in here
And your welcome in to stay
We'll serve you whiskey, stout or beer
As long as you can pay"

One large man with a farmer's brogue
Chuckled on his stool
"Your not a lad from round these parts"
Said another playing pool

"I've just moved in along the road"
To the stranger I replied
I need a place for a couple of ales
To heat me up inside

I stayed for one, then two, three, four
And then a Guinness Brian did pour
I think I had a couple more
Then after that I lost the score

I wandered home along the lane
And left the pub behind
And swore I'd be back in again
For no better house you'll find

The Gleared Eye Optimist

Carry me homeward faithful friend
From the bright lights on the hill
With miles until our journey's end
For I have had my fill

The stumbling stance of heavy tread
Weighted down with ale and gin
Help me to my darlings bed
Where she does rest within

And she will greet me with a smile
To ease my aching heap
Hold me in her arms a while
Until I drift to sleep

Stand me up as I locate
A key to fit the door
I left the house at five past eight
And now it's ten past four

Such joy will full my honey's heart
When my scent does fill the room
For she'll inhale my fresh kebab
And public house perfume

Oh to feel my Carlsberg breath
Gently brush her neck
But I am such a caring soul
My love I shall not wake

The Golden Bond Of Marriage

The golden bond of marriage
Rolled several times around
Then with deafening silence
Rested on the ground

The wide eyed frozen children
With ketchup painted lips
Left aside their burgers
Nuggets and large chips

The Art Deco surroundings
No strangers to this sight
Witnessed broken Petra
As she ran into the night

Then one girl looked at one boy
As another, scared to cry
Said "that's just our mother"
To a lonesome passerby

Then with a swish our hero
Was standing at the door
Scarred by her reaction
She pounded cross the floor

"Once again your squealing
Has pushed me just too far,
Grab that quarter pounder
And meet me in the car"

And as they all departed
With their goods priced eighteen pound
Petra's golden marriage bond
Lay lifeless on the ground

The Hired Help's

I placed an ad in the local press
For some help around the place
My bones and back are getting soreI
There's tiredness on my face

I outlined all the skills required
And the tasks required to do
Don't think it is a one man job
May even stretch to two

Some help around the garden
Trim the trees and cut the grass
Some bags of bottles to the dump
Mostly plastic and mixed glass

We'll need someone mop the floor
And do a general clean
Hoover up and bleach the bog
Spray some Mr Sheen

The kids will need delivered
To a multitude of sites
It's an early start on Saturday
So give up your Friday nights

Odd jobs as and when are yours
To hammer, nail and screw
In wind and rain in the dead of night
I'm afraid it's up to you

And if the kids are feeling sick
Or cannot get to sleep
It's you they call to act as nurse
So don't turn off the bleep

Theres dirty plates under the bed
With food several days old
The kids wear jumpers in the sun
And bikini's when it's cold

All washing, ironing, hanging up
Feeding, baths and showers
You'll get no summer holidays
On-call twenty four hours

The pay I haven't mentioned yet
It's really rather bad
The title of this hired help post
Let's call it Mum and Dad

The Importance Of Going To Sleep On Christmas Eve

I swear when I was just a lad I woke in the dead of night
For the sound of a hoof on a slated roof
Gave me such a fright

As I lay in bed in fearful dread I gripped the blankets tight
Till a bearded man in a big red suit
Slowly came in sight

I ran with haste to the window pain
And wiped the frosted glass, to see a man from the Christmas card
Park his sleigh upon on the grass

He noticed not my transfixed stare, nor heard my trembling skin
But I watched as he entered my neighbour's house
And left a gift within

Then in an instant he appeared standing by our tree
He took from his suit a pocket watch
As the clock struck half past three

He looked so sad, then shook his head
And to his herd did say, "Alas, there's a young boy not in bed
He'll get no treats today"

Then in a flash of morning light I opened up my eyes
And saw my name, on boxes stacked
Much to my surprise

The Man in Grey

There stands a man on Portstewart prom
With a tin hat and a gun
He always there in wind and rain
Which couldn't be much fun

The seagulls fly above him
And sea spray wets his eye
Young couples sit upon his step
And watch the world go by

I've never really took the time
To find out where he's been
I know he fought in world war 1
For his country and his King

I've passed him by a thousand times
Though never once looked back
I couldn't tell you any name
That's etched upon the plaque

He's seen you stagger from the pub
And never said a word
Watched you drop your battered lad
As you stumble on the kerb

And many young romantics
Have cuddled neath his stare
Memories are flooding back
Although I won't go there

As I look back upon my youth
In truth I have to say
The prom would never feel the same
Without the man in grey

The Man Who One Time Lifted Me In Air

The man who one time lifted me in air
Leans toward and calls me close to ear
Childlike innocence etched on weather beaten face
Then reality and reason disappear

I watch him fight the demons hid within
As life and love he struggles to retrace
Confusion now tattooed upon his skin
Familiarity is soon displaced

Mother steadfast and protective in despair
Hides from life inevitable truth
Offering up on high continuous prayer
To free the man who loved her from his youth

Dust has settled and mourner slipped away
Buried deep in sorrow one will find
Recollections born from joyful day
To comfort those my father left behind

The Men Who Walk In Shadows

Time has no reason in my mind
As I stumble through each day
While others dream in colour
My thoughts are black and grey

In endless tunnel walk with me
While reaching out a hand
I'm drowning in deep water here
Without a sight of land

From behind the clouded pane
I watch clothed skins pass by
Their journeys routine and mundane
Below a charcoal sky

What devils come to call my name
As I sit here in my chair
The vultures circle high above
To feast on my despair

A photograph floats to the floor
Wherein an image glows
Recalling once a happy day
A time before the shadow

The Path of Life

I wander down the Path of Life
Through forest, glen and stream
Embrace the cool fresh mountain air
And drift into my dream

With loved ones on a distant beach
The waves at my command
The warming brush of midday sun
On untouched golden sand

This picture painted in a book
Reflects my perfect land
But often on this Path of Life
Reality deals her hand

She brings us all back down to earth
For with fears the road is lined
And plays the most unfeeling cards
To the young and vulnerable mind

She conjures up her magic
In the darkest times of all
And watches with a knowing grin
As her victims choose to fall

So pause to think before you write
From the safety of your bed
Take time to see somebody's heart
When the view you post is read

This journey on The Path of Life
Can not be travelled light
Takes bravery hope and courage
To put the ills to right

This path is so congested
With so many feet to take
But walk it with your head held high
For we all make a mistake

The Pondering Of A Twelve Year Old Boy

This strange familiarity
I feel within my head
Has led me to seek refuge
In the comfort of my bed

To escape my little brother
And the need to eat my greens
The ramblings of my mother
And my sisters Yankee dreams

My mind is changing focus
From the posters that I bought
To the question of attraction
And strange wee hairs I've got

I look at the reflection
Of someone I've only met
Whose skin is hard and pimply
And hair all styled and wet

Those once unmentioned species
We referred to as "the girls"
Now occupy some brain space
With their looks, their laughs their twirls

But though I fight these feelings
And seek solace in my books
My eyes are soon distracted
To the way her body looks

I laugh at fathers comments
"Catch someone like your mum
Pretty good to look at,
And likes a bit of fun"

So here I sit and ponder
All the treats that lie in store
The weird world they call romance
That's lives beyond my door

The Pub of The Dead
(Sometimes when your sitting looking at the bottom of a glass all you
can see is the table)

Silent afternoon reflection
Is disturbed by stumbled pass
And the muffled interruption
Of the crash of tile on glass

As the change of head direction
And the individual gasp
Of the stranger in the corner
And the tenders sharp lambast

Ghostly calm is reinstated
Debris swept from cold tile floor
Blue smoke blanket hangs like sea mist
In the post war grey decor

Sporting pages are unfolded
And selections picked once more
Coins rotated on the table
Prior to walking to the door

Of this room the storytellers
Have recited gruesome calls
Of the young men who in bravery
Lost their hearts within these walls

Is a place where dreams are broken
To where many souls have fled
As they sit with empty glasses
In a pub they named the Dead

The Recovery Has Been Painful

The recovery has been painful
And very slow to pass
The barbecue on Friday night
Was liquid based and fast

The dark clouds that had hovered
Through the breaking of the day
Had drifted off to Lisburn
And to the sun gave way

The hostess in the parlour
Finished off with dainty touch
The master of the fork and tong
Complained " You've made too much".

The red carpet was rolled out
As the chosen few arrived
We're asked to keep their coats on
And find a pew outside

Some looked confused and puzzled
And were slow to take their seat
They hung around the Maxi grill
The only source of heat

The serving wench then set about
Dishing out the treat
A feast of tender chicken breast
Sausages and meat

Salads doused in Steve McQueen
Garlic spuds and chips
Then Phyllis got the cheese cake out
And we all licked our lips

The formalities completed
The children amply fed
The adults then prioritised
Getting off their head

The bottle caps were rattled
And the vino river flowed
Personalities dissected
As the charcoal dimly glowed

The time passed by as quickly
As the clouds above our heads
But laughter and good friendship
Kept us from our beds

Alas the sleep engulfed us
And the nighttime had it's way
The taxi cabs were telephoned
And the guests all slipped away

So recovery has been painful
And very slow to pass
But the crack we had on Friday night
Will in my memory last

The Rods

I love my little darling wife
She's very seldom wrong
When entering the room last night
She sensed a foreign pong

My biggest fear it was confirmed
When getting up this morn
With bits of bog roll on the grass
I knew the drains had gone

I cursed the blasted hand wipe
And looked up to the Gods
Then donned my old green wellies
And went to get the rods

When lifting up the cover
Was met with quite a sight
The remains of a turkey stew
We had on Boxing night

Well furiously I huffed and puffed
To budge the stubborn grit
I flushed and poked with a big long stick
But it wouldn't move a bit

At last I heard a welcome whoosh
And knew the war was won
But based on what I saw today
It's bran for everyone

The Room

There is but one room in this home
Decked out in finest silver chrome
Where one can sit and ponder life
Free from kids and darling wife

Here wars and conflict don't exist
Papers are read before your missed
And you can drift upon the breeze
While trousers hang below your knees

I've always time to contemplate
Things I love and those I hate
There's comfort in the cold tiled floor
And peace behind the toilet door

Some days I've stayed for near an hour
And dreamt about it in the car
Until my legs seized up with cramp
And in a panic had to stamp

But now a rival eyes my chair
And when I go he's always there
With football magazines to read
And like his dad he does lack speed

Now I must sit in our en suite
Where things are girlie, soft and neat
And scented candle fills the air
Here when I pee, I must take care

The Walker

I walk until I cannot walk no more
Then huddle down for rest
In cold shop door
Till dawn does come
And new deliveries made
As into daily city life I fade

My blank expression cloaks a thousand screams
For just as you
I once had hopes and dreams
What brought me here to lie beneath this wall
No matter how I try i can't recall

Alas my stained and hooded combat green
Fits not the glossy profile cosmo scene
And turns folk off their afternoon cuisine
So I oblige and choose to stay unseen

And so in light I slowly walk and stare
Though few will see me, for I am not there
My history book floats gently on the air
There is no one to whom I can compare

The Wind Is Now The Master Of The Night

The Wind is now the Master of the Night
And leaves his ruthless mark upon the land
Uproots that which previously stood upright
Obedience and fear he doth demand

The deep and eerie blue respect his call
And rise at the behest of his command
Against the blackened cliff his thunder fall
His ghostly shadows dance upon the sand

No heed give he to frightened children cry
And taps a beat on roof and window glass
As images are conjured where they lye
We pray that morning come and darkness pass

"Thee Lighters Ferra Pound"

I took a day off work today
Went shopping with my wife
And came upon a magic world
Unknown in my life

A cavalcade of bargains
I'd never seen before
Soap, and tools and chocolates
All piled high on the floor

"Out of date?" you ask me
"Oh no, that's not the case"
Just rows and rows of goodies
Stacked high all ore the place

There's grass seed for the garden
And pet food for the dog
All sorts of tools and gadgets
And candles for the bog

There's multi packs of batteries
Plugs and shaving foam
Rugs and mugs and light bulbs
To decorate your home

There's sprays and creams and perfume
To chase the smells away
Special little trinkets
To make the perfect day

There's toys and books and pencils
On every isle a deal
Beans and processed tins of ham
Now that's a tasty meal

There's rows of broken biscuits
And loads of fizzy pop
Every shelf a treasure
From the bottom to the top

In such a wondrous haven
I'd love to spend the day
And everything's a quid you know
That's what the staff all say

Pile it high and sell it cheap
The only show in town
They've got us all now crying out
" Thee lighters ferra pound"

There Ain't A lot Of Gerry's Round These Days

The title that we place upon our kids
Has changed it's style in oh so many ways
But something that I ponder as I sit
Is the blatant lack of people called Gerry

This famous name once held with such regard
Was worn by my own departed dad
But now it seems resigned to middle rank
Sandwiched twixt a Kennedy or Brad

Famous men who wore the name with pride
Would look upon this trend with such disgust
And maybe even think of a campaign
To lift this solid name out of the dust

And even on our screens its been replaced
While feline co star Tom stays on the chart
No Geraldo, Gerard or Jerry for our kids
They're pushed aside by Homer, Mo and Bart

So spare a loving thought sometime today
When greeting those whose breed are in decline
And say a prayer to comfort their dismay
To see a load of Gerry's in our time

Top House Memories

On winter nights on Portstewart Strand
As the waves brush on the shore
It's said you'll hear a ghostly voice
Crying out for more

Some say it is a spirit
Who treads the ocean floor
The lost soul of a fisherman
Who casts his net no more

The locals tell a different tale
Of whom the banshee mocks
Tis he who placed the magnet
Near Jimmy's music box

The sea did crash its fist of hate
Upon the moonlit sand
As down the road in Murphy's Bar
Played Jimmy's dancing band

It was their dream to take the stage
Though none could play a note
But Top House ale and Haughey's tape
Kept the gig afloat

The fans began their dancing
The night was going to plan
But backstage crept a figure
With a magnet in his hand

The music stopped a playing
There seemed no clear escape
The Dancers hadn't brought with them
A second mixing tape

The crowd were getting restless
They'd want their money back
Then three old music hero's
Staggered from the pack

Poko, Bunt and JD
Came to save the day
And with the Illustrious Celtic Dancers
"A Pair of Brown Eyes" they did play

Now the waves are lying silent
The music plays no more
That night is but a memory
Washed up on Portstewart shore

Two Aul Men

Two aul men sit chewing the cud
Watching the day pass by
Not a word is said but a knowing look
And the pause of a lasting sigh

The relentless purr of a tractor meet
As red diesel fill the air
But the two aul men on a wooden floor
In silence sit and stare

The gentle breeze of an eastern wind
Parts their greying hair
But the two aul men in their thoughts are deep
Though no words they need to share

Some time the two have sat and watched
As youth pass through their way
Without a breath these two are one
Their look enough to say

But age, ill health and time has come
Though faithful to the end
I'll sit and chew with this aul guy
He has been my best friend

Vanity Is No Longer My Co- Pilot

Vanity is no longer my co pilot
She has spread her wings and flown
Packed up all scents and waxes
And left me on my own

The styling gels sit lifeless
With finger print engraved
The creams designed to stem the tide
Concede what can't be saved

The jeans with knee side pockets
Hang with patience on a hook
The once designer paisley shirt
No longer gets a look

The shoes that lit the dance floor
Are flung below the stairs
The Jacket that once carried dreams
Now gathers doggy hairs

The mirror we once worshiped
Gets more vengeful day by day
With HD like precision
She magnifies the grey

And those who did advise us
On what we want to wear
Now show us to a different isle
Of slack with pleated flare

So you who's bodies cling to
The fashions of the past
Embrace the woollen cardigan
The looks are fading fast

We Use To Play Outside

We use to play outside
On street in field or shore
From break of early morn
Till called from backyard door

On rocks drenched black with spray
With rods cast out we stand
Till darkness came our way
And forced us back to land

We'd run with ball and stick
Till sweat broke up our play
To Dave's to quench our thirst
Then back without delay

In teams twenty or more
We graced the Warren grass
Our dream a chance to score
Or play the perfect pass

We walked from town to strand
For golden dune we crave
With towel and coin in hand
Atlantic chill we brave

We use to play outside
On bike or board or skate
From school bell until tea
Then after until late

What A Great Place To Grow Up

If I could still remember
Most of what I have forgot
I'd still have time to sit and think
Of the memories that I've got

Of the misty nights in Portstewart
When the street lights all went out
And we kept the gang together
With a whistle and a shout

Of the twenty aside matches
That had lasted all day long
For religion didn't matter
When you set foot on the Warren

And the smoke filled days of snooker
As it hung ore the green baize
In the back room of the Monty
I recall in fondest ways

On the Old Course in the summer
When the tourists came to town
Selling used balls to the golfers
Seven Top Flight for a pound

And the music was much cooler
We had Ska, the mods and punk
Those heavy metal rockers
And some U. S. deep base funk

Local guys were all our hero's
As they filled the halls and bars
With their rock n rolling music
Beating out from their guitars

Poko, Bunt and JD
Pip and Tommy Vance
In the Top House of an evening
They could lift the dead to dance

For that place has had its front men
Who propelled the local scene
Kieran in his black attire
Was as strong as there has been

Yes the eighties were a busy time
In the Anchor we did sup
As Margaret shouted "time to go"
'Twas a great place to grow up

Zzzzzzz

I have been invaded by
Two creatures from the deep
Who have stolen all the blankets
And deprived me of my sleep

With constant jerky movements
And the stretching of their legs
The coughs, the sighs and sniffing
And the smell of rotten eggs

I am pushed like dirty laundry
To the edges of the bed
There is no chance of a pillow
Resting softly neath my head

As I rant the creatures smelly feet
Have brushed against my face
The other one is shifting shapes
And moving round the place

They now have come to settle
And are static for a while
The light projected from my phone
Reflects their peaceful smile

I'll sit awake till morning
Or on the carpet lye
To know my little creatures
Sleep happily close by

ABOUT THE AUTHOR

Pablo Doherty is an Irish author who was raised in Portstewart County Derry, studied in Liverpool England and now lives outside Lurgan, County Armagh. He is married with four children without whom there would be no point.

11959514R00058

Printed in Great Britain
by Amazon.co.uk, Ltd.,
Marston Gate.